Israel and the Land Promise in Biblical Prophecy © 2025 by David Campbell

All rights reserved. No part of this publication may be reproduced, distributed, or transmitted in any form or by any means, including photocopying, recording, or other electronic or mechanical methods, without the prior written permission of the publisher or author, except in the case of brief quotations embodied in critical reviews and certain other noncommercial uses permitted by copyright law. For permission requests, email the publisher or author at addresses below:

Contact the author:
www.davidhcampbell.com

Contact the publisher:
David Campbell Christian Publishing
trinitycc@rogers.com

Scripture quotations are from the ESV® Bible (The Holy Bible, English Standard Version®), copyright © 2001 by Crossway, a publishing ministry of Good News Publishers. Used by permission. All rights reserved.

ISBN-978-1-0693289-2-2

Printed in the United States of America
Ingram Printing & Distribution, 2025

First Edition

 Christian Publishing

ISRAEL
AND THE LAND PROMISE
IN BIBLICAL PROPHECY

DAVID CAMPBELL

TABLE OF CONTENTS

Author's Preface   1
Introduction   5

PART ONE: *The Jewish people and the state of Israel in Biblical perspective*

    1 Dispensationalism and the restoration of the state of Israel   11

    2 God's plan for the Jewish people   23

    3 The state of Israel and the land promise   39

PART TWO: *The land promise in the Old Testament*

    4 Eden and the temple of the Garden   49

    5 The land promise to Abraham   57

    6 The rise and fall of Israel   65

    7 The prophets and the restoration of Israel   73

PART THREE: *The land promise in the New Testament*

    8 The land promise in Matthew   91

    9 The land promise in Hebrews and Paul   103

    10 The land promise in Revelation   111

Conclusion   119
About the Author   123

AUTHOR'S PREFACE

Many years ago when I was a seminary student, a good friend said to me, "Your eschatology affects everything you believe." His comment, while not provoking me to study as it ought to have done, nevertheless stayed with me. Today I realize how right he was. And to his original observation I would add the following, "Your lack of eschatology equally affects everything you believe."

This is the second in a series of three books in which I try to make up for the ground lost in my earlier years. The first book, called *Mystery Explained*, is a simple verse by verse guide to Revelation. This book deals with the question of whether the land promise given to Abraham finds its Biblical fulfillment in the restoration of the modern state of Israel, and the nature of God's continuing commitment to the Jewish people. The last book will deal with a whole range of eschatology hot topics from the mark of the beast to the millennium, most of which generate far more heat than light in popular discussion. All three books are designed to be readable by the average person, while still covering all the Biblical bases in a comprehensive manner.

This is not an academic book which requires citation of sources, but I would recommend in particular several books which have helped and influenced me in the preparation of this study:

G.K. Beale, *A New Testament Biblical Theology: The transformation of the Old Testament in the New* (2011)

G.K. Beale and David H. Campbell, *Revelation: A Shorter Commentary* (2014)

G.K. Beale, *The Book of Revelation* (1999)

G.K. Beale, *The Temple and the Church's Mission: A Biblical theology of the dwelling place of God* (2004)

Oren T. Martin, *Bound for the Promised Land: The land promise in God's redemptive plan* (2015)

Thanks again to Owen Woltjer and his company David and Brook, for producing this book, and for the technical support of my friend Josh Best, who has helped me get all my books to market.

A special thanks to Pastor Alex and Diana Sagot and Calvary Church Miami for financially supporting production of this book.

As always, my greatest debt is to my wife Elaine, who has stood alongside me in the work of the kingdom for over forty years.

Soli Deo gloria — glory to God alone.

INTRODUCTION

Ever since the establishment of the modern state of Israel in 1948, Christians have struggled to understand whether or not Israel as a political entity represents the fulfillment of Biblical prophecy, and if so, whether it is the duty of Christians to support Israel regardless of its actions or the fact it is in general a nation composed largely of unbelieving secularists and ultra-religious orthodox Jews, with a very small number of followers of Christ.

Christians have believed since Paul's statement at the end of Romans 11 that God has a plan to save and restore many among the Jewish people. But the Jewish people can hardly be equated with the political state of Israel, and it cannot be argued that the saving promises of God are to be extended to any political entity, whether Israel or any other nation.

Our efforts to find appropriate ways of response as Christians to developments in the middle east have been enormously complicated and distorted by the popularity of a system of teaching known as dispensationalism. This system is a relatively modern novelty, dating to the year 1828 and a British Bible teacher called J.N. Darby, who was obsessed with the idea that God would restore the nation of Israel as a political entity and made it a cornerstone of his prophetic plan. Before 1828, the ideas promoted by Darby and his subsequent followers were more or less unknown in the history of the church. In more recent years, this system has been popularized by writers such as Hal Lindsey and the Left Behind series of novels and films. Its truths have been taken for granted by people who have no idea what the system as a whole teaches.

The idea that Biblical prophecy is fulfilled in the establishment of the state of Israel in 1948 is at the very heart of dispensationalist teaching. And the basis for it is found by its followers in the contention that the state of Israel is the fulfillment of the promise of the land originally given to Abraham and reaffirmed subsequently in the Old Testament. The land promise is without argument a consistent theme of the Old Testament. The question is what the meaning of that promise is both in the Old Testament itself, and subsequently in the New Testament in light of the work of Christ. That, along with the nature of God's concern for the Jewish people, is what we seek to explain in this short book.

PART ONE

THE JEWISH PEOPLE AND THE STATE OF ISRAEL IN BIBLICAL PERSPECTIVE

CHAPTER ONE

DISPENSATIONALISM AND THE RESTORATION OF THE STATE OF ISRAEL

In 1828, J.N. Darby held a series of prophetic conferences in which he developed the view that God had two covenant peoples, Jews and Christians. Darby saw the Bible as divided into strict time periods or "dispensations" during which God dealt differently with humanity. God dealt with the Jews through the law, for instance, and with the church through grace. The time periods and modes of God's dealing are clearly set forth and cannot be mixed — in any given period of history, God can only deal with one people one way. According to Darby's system, God's intention in sending Christ to earth was to fulfill God's promise to David that his descendants would rule over an eternal earthly kingdom.

Unexpectedly, the Jewish people rejected God's offer and crucified the Messiah instead. God was now faced with a problem. He resorted to Plan B. He raised Jesus from the dead, and created the church. The church was not his original purpose, but exists as a "parenthesis" in the divine plan, which is still centered on Israel.

The problem Darby created for himself is that in his system God is left, so to speak, with two distinct covenant peoples, Israel and the church, and two distinct ways of dealing with them, law and grace. The dispensations cannot overlap. For Darby, who was interested above all in the restoration of Israel, Jesus' original mission was in some way a failure. God had left the Jewish people hanging, and now had no way of dealing with them, as he had created a new dispensation of grace. The only solution would be to find a way to remove the church entirely so that he could return to his original, and central mission, the mission Jesus had failed to accomplish, to fulfill Old Testament prophecy by the restoration not only of the state of Israel but of the whole Old Testament sacrificial system, and to install Christ over its operation. In his conferences between 1828 and 1930, this removal of the church was the critical missing piece.

But then a fortuitous event took place. In 1830, a young woman in Scotland called Margaret MacDonald had joined a sect called the Irvingites, followers of a man called Edward Irving, who in some ways were forerunners of the modern charismatic movement, but with some strange doctrinal twists. In an Irvingite prayer meeting, Margaret MacDonald had a vision concerting the events leading up to the return of Christ. She wrote these words: "Only those who have the light of God within them will see the sign of his appearance… 'tis only those that are alive in him that will be caught up to meet him in the air." No one was quite sure what the vision meant. Until it reached Darby.

Darby was well informed concerning the Irvingites, and as news of this vision spread widely in Irvingite circles, it almost certainly reached Darby's ears. It is an historical fact that he knew who she was. Darby immediately provided the missing interpretation. Margaret saw something never before revealed in the entire history of the church. No one, not the church fathers, not Augustine, not Aquinas, not Calvin, Luther or Wesley had ever seen this. In fact, no theologian, Biblical teacher or church leader had ever understood the revelation now given to Darby through Margaret. What Margaret saw in the vision was a secret return of Christ, a return entirely distinct from the commonly understood Biblical teaching of his visible return.

Darby had struck oil. The vision had handed him the answer to his riddle. The purpose of this secret return, which Darby called the "rapture," was to remove the church from the world, which would then enable God to return to his original purposes and establish his covenant with the Jews. Because this entailed Christ returning to Jerusalem and ruling over an earthly restored Jewish kingdom, Darby predicted that following the secret return of Christ and removal of the church, there would follow a seven-year period of tribulation (an idea derived from a bizarre interpretation of four verses in Daniel 9), culminating in the battle of Armageddon portrayed in Rev.16:14-16. This battle would involve a coalition of pagan nations attacking a restored state of Israel. It would result in a mass conversion of Jews, and following Armageddon, Christ would establish an earthly kingdom based in Jerusalem, consisting of Jews converted in the tribulation. He identified this as the millennial period referred to in Rev. 20:1-3 and saw it lasting a literal thousand years. And his theological system, albeit erroneous, was at last complete.

And so between 1831 and 1833, Darby held a further series of conferences in which he outlined his revelation of a secret rapture to be followed by a seven year tribulation. His friend Edward Irving began teaching Darby's doctrine shortly after. Darby then superimposed this idea on the book of Revelation, supposing (as he admitted, without any foundation in the text itself) that chapters 6-19 refer to this period of tribulation, and disregarding John's own clear statement in 1:9 that the tribulation had already begun in John's own day. Everything in his doctrine centered on Israel, for that was Darby's obsession. The kingdom of God as portrayed in the Old Testament was completely different from the church, or anything God did through the church. When Jesus announced what the text of the Gospels indicate is the imminent or actual arrival of the kingdom, he was announcing something that in fact would not happen for over 2000 years (and counting). The kingdom would be fulfilled only in a series of events commencing in the restoration of the state of Israel. At the end of the seven year tribulation, Christ would return to earth to do what he was originally supposed to do, establish an earthly rule based in Jerusalem.

Everything in Darby's system hinged on one fact: *the promise of possession of the land of Israel*, the promise given originally to Abraham, which was fulfilled in part under Joshua, more fully under David and Solomon, which was lost in the exile, and which must be restored in order for the whole dispensational system to work. Christ must return to a Jewish Jerusalem in order at last to establish his earthly throne, rebuild the temple and re-institute the sacrificial system for a period of a literal one thousand years. But without the restoration of the state of Israel, the entire system would fail. And without the land promise as Darby interpreted it, there would be no restoration of Israel. The meaning of the land promise is thus vital to a proper interpretation of the whole substance of Biblical eschatology.

Dispensationalism has some surprising quirks. It teaches, for instance, that the Gospels are intended for the Jews only, though they may have some devotional value to Christians. The reason is that they contain Jesus' message to the Jewish people concerning the establishment of his literal earthly kingdom. The Gospels will not find fulfillment until the millennium, and then only among the Jews. And the kingdom of God, the coming of which was the central proclamation of both Jesus and the early church, is not present in the church age, in spite of the fact its arrival was the first and last thing Jesus proclaimed in his earthly ministry. The new covenant in Christ, prophesied in Jeremiah 31 and taught as fulfilled in Christ in Hebrews 8, does not fully come into effect until the millennium, but Christians in the church age are able to enjoy its benefits in advance by grace. Darby also put forth the idea of an apostolic dispensation or period of time, which ended with the completion of the New Testament canon. The miraculous manifestations of the

Spirit were intended as temporary measures to reinforce the early preaching of the church, and ceased with the writing of the last New Testament documents. It has always puzzled me why Pentecostals are often the most ardent dispensationalists, when dispensationalism itself denies everything that is at the heart of any Pentecostal or charismatic movement.

Darby's idea of the rapture spread, but not within orthodox Christianity. In the early 1840s, William Miller, co-founder of the Seventh Day Adventists, predicted that Christ would visibly return in 1844. When this did not happen, he declared that Christ had invisibly entered the heavenly sanctuary to commence the process of eternal judgment. Mormonism, birthed at almost exactly the same time, though not accepting the secret rapture, endorsed Darby's concept of a literal earthly millennium.

But perhaps the greatest consequence of Darby's ideas was their impact on Charles Taze Russell, founder of the Jehovah's Witnesses. Russell was heavily influenced by the Seventh Day Adventists and their take on the rapture, as well as their rejection of the Trinity and of a literal hell. Like Darby, he was an ardent Zionist, believing in the reestablishment of the state of Israel as a key to the return of Christ. The early title of the

Jehovah's Witnesses was Zion's Watch Tower Tract Society. Russell declared that Darby's rapture would occur in 1878, and in preparation sold all his businesses. Later, he published books in which he asserted that Christ had in fact invisibly returned in 1874 to begin the end-times harvest through the Jehovah's Witnesses. He picked up Darby's doctrine of the seven year tribulation ending in a multinational attack on a restored Israel culminating in the battle of Armageddon. He saw the outbreak of World War 1 as marking the end of the Gentile dispensation, the beginning of Armageddon and the establishment of the state of Israel. He taught that Jews did not not need to be converted, should return to Palestine and reconstitute the Biblical state of Israel, which would be the center of God's earthly kingdom. Russell also picked up Darby's ideas of dispensations. He further taught that the kingdom of God was established in heaven in 1914, to be governed by a group of 144,000 heavenly-resurrected chosen Witnesses who would work in heaven toward establishment of a millennial paradise on earth. While Russell's views do not cohere exactly with Darby's, the numerous parallels make clear his dependency on Darby's thought.

Dispensationalism was popularized with the publication of a study Bible by C.I. Scofield, an associate of D.L. Moody, in 1909. It burst into prominence further with the apparent vindication of Darby's prophecy concerning the restoration of the state of Israel in 1948. Its view of the rapture, the secret return of Christ, the tribulation and a literal thousand year millennium were entrenched by the best-selling book *The Late Great Planet Earth* by Hal Lindsey, and by the *Left Behind* books and films of Tim LaHaye and Jerry Jenkins.

Today, this understanding of eschatology is the prevailing view among Christians in North America, even if few have comprehension of its details and consequences. Many, if not most of you reading this book have, knowingly or not, allowed your understanding of the end-times to be conditioned by it.

This book was not written as a guide to politics in the middle east. It does not express approval or disapproval of the actions of any nation. That does not mean such approval or disapproval is inappropriate. It simply means that *we cannot form our judgments on the basis of a predetermined view of Biblical prophecy* which places divine approval on the state of Israel, no matter what actions or policies it pursues. Like any other nation, Israel must rise or fall morally on the basis of its own values and actions. Such judgments can be made on the basis of *Biblical ethics* — what is right and wrong —but cannot be made on the basis of *Biblical eschatology*.

We must make our case concerning whether or not the political state of Israel has any significance in Biblical prophecy from what the Bible has to say about it. But before we do that, we need to understand what the Bible has to say about the Jewish people. Has God forgotten them? Does his calling of the Jewish people since the days of Abraham still hold validity in light of the gospel? This is in fact the very question Paul faced and answered.

CHAPTER TWO

GOD'S PLAN FOR THE JEWISH PEOPLE

It is a moral given for Christians, as it should be for all people, to stand firmly against anti-semitism. We do that purely on the basis of our Christian belief in the sanctity of life. Discrimination on the basis of race, let alone genocide in never acceptable in God's sight. This is particularly so in light of the Holocaust. In Bremen, Germany, we saw the small gold-covered cobblestones placed in the pavement outside the homes of Jews who were taken away and murdered by the Nazis. In Berlin, we shuddered when we discovered that the restaurant we were eating in had been the headquarters of the Hitler Youth (and subsequently, of its Stalinist counterpart).

But antisemitism should be especially repugnant for Christians. First of all, it need scarcely be noted that Jesus himself, as well as almost all the early church leaders, were Jews. But there is another reason. Paul's teaching clearly demonstrates that God has a special plan for the Jewish people. This plan is inextricably linked to God's own faithfulness.

In Rom. 1:18-3:20, Paul has shown that all people are under judgment because of sin, so that possession of the law does not give the Jew any advantage in terms of salvation. During the course of his argument, he stops at 3:1-8 briefly to make the point that this does not cancel the faithfulness of God to the Jews, but he does not elaborate there on what he means by this. From the latter part of chapter 3 to the end of chapter 8, he explains the message of the gospel and its implications for the lives of Christian believers. But the question remains what then have become of God's promises to Israel? This, of course, was the same question Darby struggled with. If God was not faithful to those promises, why should we assume he will be faithful to the promises he has given to the church? And so in chapters 9-11, Paul develops his answer to the question he briefly introduced in 3:1-8. But unlike Darby, his answer focusses not on *the restoration of the state of Israel but on the restoration of the Jewish people.*

The topic of these chapters is the relationship of Jews and Gentiles in the plan of God, with a particular focus on the faithfulness of God in his dealings with both groups. Paul's goal is to explain how Israel is responsible for her rejection of God's promises, and yet how this will not ultimately frustrate the purposes of God for her. Along the way, he shows how Gentiles also can miss God's plan for them, and how they need to remain faithful to the Lord. By the time he gets to the end of his argument, Paul has shown God's faithfulness to Jew and Gentile alike.

In chapters 9 and 10, he describes at length how the Jewish people rejected their Messiah, and how the gospel was received instead by the Gentiles. He shows how Scripture itself prophesies this would happen. After all Paul has said about the disobedience of Israel in chapters 9 and 10, he now asks whether this means God has rejected his people (11:1-6). To this the answer is no. God's choice of Paul is itself a demonstration of that (verse 1). If God can save Paul, who was a persecutor of Christians, then there surely must still be hope for other Jews. Therefore, quoting 1 Sam. 12:22, he declares that God "has not rejected his people whom he foreknew" (verse 2a). Samuel was rebuking the Israelites for disobedience, while assuring them that God would not abandon them. Likewise, Paul's reference to God's reply to Elijah's complaint (1 Kgs. 19:18) in verses 2b-4, points back to a time of spiritual decline when the prophet feared he was the only faithful one left in the land. Paul must fear the same, yet Elijah's story encourages him that God has others yet to save among the Jewish people. This remnant is chosen by God's grace alone, not by human works or merit (verses 5-6). Unconditional election cannot be intermixed with any form of human works. For Paul, the purity of grace means that God elects without human works. Without unconditional election, Paul's doctrine of justification by faith cannot stand.

Paul summarizes his discussion on the disobedience of Israel in 11:7-10. Israel failed to attain what they sought; in spite of the fact they had heard the gospel message, they determined to pursue righteousness by law instead of by faith. Instead, according to the Greek text, "election [not "the elect" as in ESV] has obtained it" (verse 7). Paul could easily have written "the elect," but he did not. His use of "election" highlights the work of God alone in enabling fallen humanity to reach righteousness by faith. Apart from the chosen remnant of Israel, the rest were hardened (verse 7). This concept is hard for us to understand, but it does not exempt humanity from responsibility. It may be a mystery to our limited rationality how divine sovereignty and human free will can work together, but the Bible resolves it by the understanding that it is God, in his sovereignty, who grants us free will. Theologically, this is known as compatibilism: the sovereignty of God and the free will of humanity work together, though on the understanding that free will only comes as a gift of God. They are not equally balanced factors, for that would mean God is no longer the sovereign Creator God of the Bible, but a being reduced by the independent operation of human beings. Human free will operates, as one commentator puts it, under the umbrella of the sovereignty of God.

God has hardened those who were already sinners in the same way he hardened Pharaoh, so even the hardening is a form of judgment. Paul supports this in verses 8-10 by quotations from all three parts of the Hebrew Bible, the Torah (Deut. 29:4), the Prophets (Isa. 29:10) and the Writings (Ps. 69:22-23). The context in Deuteronomy is interesting, because in it Moses acknowledges the Israelites are incapable of obeying the law "until this day" (Deut. 29:3), but goes on in Deut. 30:6 to tell of the day of their deliverance when God will circumcise their hearts. Paul has spoken of the hardening of the Jews until his own day, but like Moses, will go on in the rest of the chapter to speak of a future time of deliverance.

The rest of chapter 11 is taken up with Paul's discussion of salvation history. In 11:11-16, he shows how Israel's hardening has resulted in salvation for the Gentiles. The trespass of the Jews has led to the Gentiles being saved (verse 11). But if their failure has meant riches for the

Gentiles, how much more powerful will be the impact of their own "inclusion" or "fullness" (verse 12). The word "fullness" is the Greek word *pleroma*. When we compare this with the statement in verse 25 of the time when the "fullness" of the Gentiles has come in, it seems the word "fullness" is equivalent to "the full number." For now, Paul is advertising his ministry to the Gentiles in the hope that it will stir up a sense of godly jealousy among the Jews to reclaim their heritage (verses 13-14). But a time will come when, by contrast with the present season of hardening, the Jews will turn to the Messiah in great numbers or "fullness." This is further defined in verse 15 as the time of their "acceptance" by God, as opposed to the present season of their "rejection." If even the time of their rejection has resulted in reconciliation for the world (the Gentiles coming to Christ), then the time of their acceptance will amount to "life from the dead."

In verse 16, Paul states that if the first fruits are holy, so is the whole lump, and if the root is holy, so are the branches. The first fruits and the root must be identified with the patriarchs, the faithful fathers of the Jewish people, and the promises given to them that in Israel all the nations of the earth would be blessed. But if the first fruits are holy, so is the rest. This can only refer to God's election of Israel as a people. This does not contradict Paul's argument in 9:6-13 that ethnic and spiritual Israel are two different entities, nor does it negate the fact that there is at present only a remnant of Jews who remain faithful. God chooses to save some Israelites but not others. Yet he has not forsaken the people as a whole, and the proof of this is that he has reserved a great harvest among them before the Lord returns, as the following verses will indicate.

In light of this, Paul must warn the Gentile converts against boasting (11:17-22). The Gentiles have been grafted in as wild shoots into the nourishing root of the olive tree, a figure of speech used to describe Israel in the Old Testament (Jer. 11:16-19; Hos. 14:6-7). It is true that some of the natural branches have been removed because of their failure to believe in Christ (verse 17). The olive tree cannot be identified here as national Israel in the same sense it was in the Old Testament, however, because Paul has already spoken of how many of its branches have been cut off — most, in fact. But it does represent the *faithful remnant* descended from the patriarchs, and as such constitutes the original tree into which the Gentile converts have been grafted. The Gentiles have not been grafted into Israel understood as a political state, or even as an ethnic group. They have been grafted into the *faithful remnant* of Israel. The result is the faithful people of God, Jew and Gentile alike. But in this Paul is concerned to make the point that this falling away by most Jews and the grafting in of many Gentiles *does not annul the fact that the olive tree (the faithful*

Jewish remnant) still exists. And so the Gentiles must avoid any boasting (verses 18-21).

He has warned the Jews of the foolishness of boasting in their own advantages (2:1-3:20). Now he warns the Gentile converts also. Their inclusion is purely by the grace of God. And the same God who cut off the natural branches will not hesitate to cut off those grafted in if they are unfaithful. The Gentiles should consider both the severity and the kindness of God (verse 22). We cannot appreciate the kindness of God in saving us by grace unless we also consider the severity of the judgment of God toward those who are disobedient. None of us are worthy of his grace. If Gentiles do not continue in the kindness of God, they will be cut off. Paul is not talking here about genuine believers losing their salvation. He is addressing the realities of the visible church, a church in which there is always a mixture of truly saved and merely professing believers. Gentile members cannot presume they are saved simply because they see themselves as superior to the apostate Jewish community around them. They are saved only because they have had a personal encounter with Christ and are engaged with him in a living relationship of faith. As time passes, churches may become lukewarm or even apostate, and Paul's warnings will come to pass. These warnings are directed toward the church of every generation. The same phenomenon explains the warnings against falling away in the letter to the Hebrews. Paul teaches that we must continually exercise faith in God and remain faithful to his calling; we must work out our salvation with fear and trembling (Phil. 2:12). Again, this does not imply that the elect, those truly chosen and saved by God, can or will lose their salvation. Those who fail to persevere reveal the fact they were never truly saved to begin with (1 Jn. 2:19).

In 11:23-27, Paul reaches the climax of his message. Israel, as the natural branches, can certainly be grafted back into the natural tree, which is the faithful remnant (verses 23-24). The condition is that they no longer continue in their unbelief. Paul nowhere teaches that any Jewish person can be saved without genuine repentance and faith in the Messiah. But Paul wishes to impart a "mystery" to his Gentile hearers so that they do not become proud (verse 25a). By "mystery" he does not mean some kind of divine riddle beyond human understanding. According to the New Testament, a "mystery" is a secret element in God's plan that was previously hidden but has now been revealed. Paul uses the word in this sense quite often (Rom. 16:25; 1 Cor. 2:1; Eph. 1:9 Col. 1:26; 2 Thess. 2:7; 1 Tim. 3:9). The "mystery" in Paul usually refers to the gospel itself. In Revelation, the word has the sense of something hidden in God's plan but now fulfilled in an unexpected manner, with particular reference to the work of Christ. This is part of what Paul also means, in that Christ came unexpectedly not as a conquering king, but as a suffering servant who exercised authority over the entire course of history by hanging helpless on a Roman cross.

But the mysterious aspect of the plan of God Paul is unveiling in this passage deals with the unfolding of God's plan in history in relation to the Jewish people. The content of the mystery is that Israel's hardening is for a limited period of time, the salvation of the Gentiles will precede the salvation of Israel, and that "all Israel" will eventually be saved (verses 25b-27). He has previously spoken of the future "fullness" of Israel (11:12), of the coming time of their "acceptance" (11:15), and of their being grafted back into their own olive tree (11:24). The "mystery" speaks of a future time in which the Jews, after all their centuries of rejecting the gospel, will unexpectedly turn to the Messiah. *This salvation, however, does not occur outside of faith in Christ. Israel is held accountable for failing to believe in Christ* (9:31-10:8). Salvation for Jews and Gentiles comes only through faith in Christ (10:9-13). Paul is an example of the saved Jewish remnant only because he believes in Christ (11:1-6). There is no salvation for Israel outside of believing in Jesus the Messiah. Nor does Paul speak here of Jews hardened throughout past history being somehow retroactively saved at the end of history, as if all Jews of all times are going to be saved irrespective of faith in Christ. People are objects of God's blessings or his wrath. Hardened Jews are objects of

God's wrath and cannot be saved (9:23-24, 27-29). Here Paul is speaking of something which has not yet happened.

What is yet to come, therefore, is that "all Israel" will be saved (verse 26). What does this mean? What is referred to here by "Israel?" Paul says clearly that Christian believers are the true Jews (Rom. 2:28-29; Phil. 3:3), the sons and daughters of Abraham (Rom. 4:1-17; Gal. 3:6-9, 26-29) and the Israel of God (Gal. 6:16). And it is clear that Gentiles are included in the number of God's chosen people in the passage in Hosea quoted in 9:24-26 (those who are not God's people will be sons of the living God). So it would not be out of line to think he is talking here about the church, composed of Jewish and Gentile believers. The problem, however, is that in verse 25 Paul has clearly referred to ethnic Israel being hardened, and so it is highly likely that when he uses the word "Israel" in the very next verse, the meaning is the same. So "all Israel" in this text must refer to ethnic Jews.

Some have understood the passage to mean that once the fullness of the Gentiles has come in, then whatever might be needed to make up the remnant of saved ethnic Jews will be completed. But this causes the passage to end in a massive anti-climax. Paul has spoken of a future "fullness" of the Jews, just has there is now for the Gentiles (verse 12). He has talked about their present decisive rejection as contrasted with their future decisive acceptance (verse 14).

He has spoken of a present breaking off in contrast with a future grafting in (verses 20-24). Clearly he is referring to a time of great revival among the Jewish people. The period of hardening of the Jews will end when the fullness of the Gentiles has been completed (verse 25). The phrase "all Israel will be saved" refers to a massive turning to Christ among the Jewish people in the very last days before the Lord's return. "All" does not necessarily represent every last Jew living at the time, but that such a great percentage will be saved that an observer could easily say, "All Israel has been saved."

The climax of this revival will be the return of the Lord, when "the Deliverer will come from Zion" (verse 27). The Scriptures quoted in verses 26-27 (Isa. 59:20; 27:9) speak of a restoration of Israel in connection with a time of judgment. The Deliverer in the Old Testament is Yahweh, but here the reference is undoubtedly to Christ and his return: "…and to wait for his Son from heaven, whom he raised from the dead, Jesus, who delivers us from the wrath to come," (1 Thess. 1:10).

This turning to the Messiah of the Jewish people and their incorporation into the body of Christ immediately prior to the one, only, visible return of the Lord is *completely different* from the dispensationalist view that the Gentiles are raptured out of this world, and Israel, restored as a nation, receives the Old Testament promises in an earthly millennium characterized by the re-institution of the law and temple sacrifices as the basis of relationship with God.

The marvellous truth is that, as one commentator puts it, God has designed history in such a way that the gift of his grace always surprises those who receive it — first Gentiles, then Jews. This again underlines the sovereignty of God in his gracious gift of salvation.

In 11:28-32, Paul summarizes God's plan. The Gentiles might have been under the impression that the Jews had little further place in God's plan, as they are "enemies as regards the gospel." But God's opposition to Israel is not the end of the story, for "as regards election, they are beloved for the sake of their forefathers" (verse 28). Election is that work by which God originally chose Israel as his people. God's gifts and calling are "irrevocable" (verse 29). This word is a legal term referring to the unbreakable nature of a commitment. The Rabbis believed that the Jewish people could bolster their standing with God by borrowing from the meritorious works of the patriarchs. But this thought is far from Paul's mind, for God chose even the patriarchs only by grace. Abraham, after all, was an idol worshipper when God met him (Josh. 24:2). God's saving of the Jews in the days before Christ's return will be as much an act of sheer grace as his saving of the Gentiles has been.

The salvation of Israel at the end of history fulfills God's gracious covenant promises to Abraham, Isaac and Jacob. The Gentiles had in the past been disobedient to God (verse 30), whereas now the Jews are (verse 31a). But the fact that the fullness of the Gentiles has begun to arrive paves the way for God also to move among the Jews (verse 31b). Paul actually says, "that they may now receive mercy" (verse 31b). The "now" sounds a bit strange given that Paul is referring to events which have not yet, even in our day, taken place. But the New Testament telescopes the whole of history commencing with the resurrection into the phrase "the last days" (Acts 2:17; Jas. 5:3; 2 Pet. 3:3; 1 Jn. 2:18), and views us as already living in them. The last days are now! With the Lord, a day is as a thousand years (2 Pet. 3:8). The harvest of the Gentiles makes it possible for God to move among the Jews at any time, the same way his return may occur at any time. No other events in redemption history need to take place before either of these things happen. This does not mean we should expect them to happen soon, just that we should live in light of the fact that they might. God's "now" and our "now" have to be understood differently.

In verse 32, Paul sums up chapters 9-11 as a whole: "For God has consigned all to disobedience, that he may have mercy on all." God has structured history in order to have mercy on all. This is not universalism. It is not *all without exception* who are saved, but *all without distinction*. God will draw his people out of every tribe, people, language and nation, just as John saw in his vision of the heavenly throne room (Rev. 7:9).

CHAPTER THREE

THE STATE OF ISRAEL AND THE LAND PROMISE

Surely, then, we might argue, in view of God's commitment to the Jewish people, he must be equally committed to the Jewish state that was established in 1948? And this is exactly what dispensationalism argues. A key tenet in dispensational theology is the unconditional nature of the land promise to Israel. God's commitment to ethnic Israel includes possession of the land promised to Abraham in perpetuity.

Let's start by looking at the extent of the land originally promised to Israel. The land promised by God to Abraham was defined in its Biblical boundaries as extending from "the river of Egypt to the great river, the river Euphrates"

(Gen. 15:18). The phrase "the river of Egypt" does not refer to the Nile (the Hebrew word for the Nile is different), but to what is called the "brook of Egypt" in Num. 34:5, likely the present-day Wadi el Arish, which flows into the Mediterranean between Israel and the Nile. Later, God told Moses the promised land would extend from the Red Sea (the present-day region of Eilat) to the Mediterranean, and from the wilderness to the Euphrates (or to nearby Mount Hor, Num. 34:7), considerably to the north-east of present-day Damascus (Exod. 23:31; Deut. 11:24; Josh. 1:4). The eastern boundary would run southward passing to the west of Damascus onward to the Sea of Galilee, and down the Jordan to the Dead Sea (Num. 34:10-12). From a present-day perspective, this would include most of Lebanon, a reasonable chunk of Syria, the Golan Heights and the West Bank, as well as Gaza — considerably more than the boundaries of present-day Israel. Nowhere does the New Testament explicitly cancel or alter this promise. It is simply silent on it, at least in explicit terms.

It is part of the foundational teaching of dispensationalism that God has two covenant peoples, Israel and the church, and there are promises to each. While dispensationalism sees the fulfillment of the land promise ultimately in the earthly millennium at which Christ will rule in Jerusalem following the rapture of the church, it also sees its preliminary fulfillment in the re-establishment of the state of Israel. That event, which took place in 1948, is seen an expression of God's blessing on his covenant people. It is also a necessary precursor to the fulfillment of Biblical prophecy. It initiates a time-line that will result in the return of Christ *within one generation,* according to the dispensationalist interpretation of Matt. 24:34: "this generation will not pass away until all these things take place." This means the church must be raptured seven years prior to that, thus initiating the prophesied seven-year tribulation during which the state of Israel will be attacked by an alliance of enemy nations.

Although this prophetic timeline has generated almost continuous predictions by dispensational teachers regarding world events and Christ's return ever since 1948, it should be obvious that time is running out on their system, even if it is clearly not running out on history as a whole. The problem for dispensationalism is obvious: one cannot keep stretching the definition of "generation" indefinitely. Dispensationalists teach that the *generation alive in 1948* will live either to be caught up in the rapture (if they are Christians) or to go through the tribulation and witness the return of Christ (if they are not). At the time of writing of this book (2025), this places *the very youngest member* of that generation at 77 years old, the vast majority have died, and we are still awaiting the rapture, let alone Christ's return. In any event, when looking at the context in Matt. 24:34 and comparing it with his use of the same word "generation" in Matt. 11:18 and 12:41, it seems clear that Jesus was referring in all three passages to the *lifetime of the people he was talking to, not of some hypothetical future generation.* To suggest that his words could be arbitrarily transferred to a generation over two thousand years in the future, whose lifetime would collectively extend to between 84 and 150+ years and counting strains all credulity.

J.N. Darby built his system of interpretation on the indispensable premise that God would re-institute the state of Israel. Without that, the whole system falls apart, for that is the event which starts the eschatological countdown. For dispensationalists, therefore (setting aside for a moment our critique of their understanding of Matt. 24:34), the events of 1948 were an emphatic confirmation of their theological system. For these reasons, dispensationalists are amongst the world's strongest supporters of the state of Israel and among the most uncritical of any actions it might take, regardless of the human consequences. Their unqualified endorsement is based on one simple fact: it is the single most important thing God has done since the cross, and (on the basis of the dual covenant theology) is perhaps of *equal significance* to the cross. One involves the covenant with the Jews, the other involves the covenant with the church. Without the influence of dispensationalism, it is doubtful many Christians would ever have attached great theological or Biblical significance to the establishment of Israel or felt necessary to provide it such unqualified support, though without doubt many would have understandably welcomed it simply on grounds of compassion for the Jewish people, especially after the horrors of the Holocaust.

For those who see dispensationalism as a false theological system invented eighteen centuries after Christ, a more nuanced view of Israel is possible. God has no favorites among nations, and every nation must be subject to the same moral criteria. Any given state merits support by Christians to the extent that it advances the cause of human dignity as expressed by Christ. This may lead to varying evaluations, but at least it involves attempting to approach issues from a truly Biblical perspective. History has taught us that when Christians or churches ally themselves too closely with any particular political state or ideological system, they are asking for trouble. Christianity at its best is what it was designed to be — a profoundly counter-cultural movement. Nowhere in the Bible is this more powerfully addressed than in its last book, where Christians are reminded that their battle is always to maintain purity and truth in the face of the devil's continuous attempts to use the power of human governments to lead them away from their commitment to Christ alone as Lord.

But here is the conundrum. Even if one rejects the rest of dispensational eschatology as the Biblical nonsense it is, it seems as if on this issue dispensationalists may have a case. The land was promised to Abraham, and the promise was confirmed to Moses and Joshua. God enabled Israel to take possession of the land through miraculous interventions, and sustained them in it as long as they were faithful. But the New Testament, as dispensationalists point out, does not appear to speak to the issue of the land. Instead, it seems to describe the fulfillment of Biblical prophecy in Christ in purely spiritual terms. The body of Christ is not assigned a piece of real estate the way Israel was. And neither, apparently, does the New Testament explicitly annul the promise given to Abraham. So, given this silence on the part of the New Testament, dispensationalists argue, do not the promises of the Old Testament regarding Israel's restoration to the land still stand? Can we not see the establishment of the state of Israel as a fulfillment of God's promises, an expression of his election of the Jewish people? After all, in Romans 11 Paul says in relation to the Jewish people that the gifts and call of God are irrevocable.

But this, we argue, does not represent an accurate reading of the New Testament, nor does it express the whole truth of what the Old Testament says either. As we shall see, a correct understanding of what the Bible says on this issue, far from being something peripheral we can agree to disagree on, is in fact central to a Biblical understanding of the purposes of God throughout history. To misunderstand the land promise in the way dispensationalists do is to lose track of the entire story line of the Bible.

And now we must provide evidence to support our position.

PART TWO

THE LAND PROMISE IN THE OLD TESTAMENT

CHAPTER FOUR

EDEN AND THE TEMPLE OF THE GARDEN

From beginning to end, the Bible is the story of God's presence. What is fascinating is how the theme of his presence runs throughout the Bible, connecting some of its greatest stories in a far closer way than we may have thought. For instance, Gen. 3:8 makes the following statement: "And they heard the sound of the Lord God walking in the garden in the cool of the day…" The same Hebrew verb, whose literal meaning is to "walk back and forth," is centuries later used by the prophet Nathan to describe the presence of God not in the garden but in the tabernacle: "Since the day I brought up the people of Israel from Egypt to this day… I have been moving about [lit: walking back and forth] in a tent [tabernacle] for my dwelling" (2 Sam. 7:6). And in the second last chapter of the Bible, John in turn draws from the days of Moses fourteen centuries earlier to describe the very same reality: "Behold, the dwelling place [tabernacle] of God is with man. He will dwell [tabernacle] with them, and they will be his people" (Rev. 21:3). The Bible begins and ends with the description of God walking back and forth in his tabernacle or dwelling place. The Bible is the story of how that presence was lost and then regained. If we do not understand how we fit into that story and what it implies for our lives, we will have lost track of the Bible's central message.

From beginning to end, God's presence is connected with land — a place where God dwells. Eden was a garden temple in which Adam and Eve were priests. God placed Adam in the Garden, in the ESV translation, to "work it and keep it". But the same Hebrew verbs are elsewhere in the Old Testament translated as to "serve and guard," and are used to describe the duty of priests in the tabernacle (Num. 3:7-8, for instance). The duty of the priests and Levites was to "serve" in the tabernacle and to "guard" against anything unclean entering the tabernacle (Num. 3:5-10), and Adam's duty was also to serve and guard — to serve God in the temple of the garden and to guard against anything unclean entering it. Just like Aaron and his sons in the tabernacle, Adam and Eve were priests in the temple of the garden where the presence of God dwelt.

But in Gen. 1:28, God gave Adam and Eve a further commission: "And God said to them, 'Be fruitful and multiply and fill the earth and subdue it...'" The means by which this goal was to be accomplished is stated in verse 27: "So God created man in his own image, in the image of God he created him; male and female he created them." Because they were created in his image, they were able to reflect and to enforce his rule over the whole earth. In other words, Adam and Eve were God's vice-rulers or vice-regents on earth. Not only were they to serve and guard within the garden, they were to extend the boundaries of the garden outward into the inhospitable lands outside — the lands into which they were eventually expelled. God's goal was that the whole creation would be rendered habitable for Adam and his descendants. This is confirmed by Isa. 45:18: "For thus says the Lord, who created the heavens... who formed the earth and made it (he established it; he did not create it empty, he formed it to be inhabited!)..." The ultimate goal of God was that, through the earth being subdued and made habitable, he himself would be glorified throughout his creation as the boundaries of his kingdom were extended and established. The kingdom rule of God, which was initially limited to the garden temple of Eden, was to be extended throughout the whole world by his image-bearers. The fact that Adam and Eve were to become "one flesh" (Gen. 2:24) further emphasizes the fact that their function as male and female involved beginning to fill the earth with people as the garden temple was extended, and there is no reason to believe that they did not have a significant number of offspring before the fall (though Genesis records by name only those born after), which in turn answers the question of where the other human beings referred to in the immediate post-fall history of Genesis 4 came from.

Eden therefore represented the original land promise of God, the place where his kingdom was to be established. It was lost through our disobedience, but at that catastrophic moment a prophetic promise came that the seed of the woman would bruise the heel of the serpent. That promise implies the restoration of what was lost, including the land. If God intended his representatives to possess all the land represented by the creation, this must also be his ultimate purpose in restoration. And this explains why, as Genesis progresses, God begins to unfold his agenda of restoring the land and establishing his kingdom.

It also explains why in Gen. 9:1,7, God commanded Noah to be fruitful and multiply and fill the earth.

It explains why in Gen. 17:2, 6 and 8, God promised Abraham that he would multiply his descendants and make him fruitful, and why in Gen. 22:17-18 God said that in Abraham's seed all the nations of the earth would be blessed. It explains why in Gen. 26:4, God told Isaac he would multiply his descendants and that all the nations of the earth would be blessed by them. It explains why in Gen. 35:11-12, God told Jacob to be fruitful and multiply, and that a company of nations would come from him. And it explains why in Gen. 47:27, it is recorded of Israel that they lived in Egypt and were fruitful and became very numerous. The elements of the commission to Adam (to be fruitful and multiply and to fill the earth) are repeated over and over again from Noah through Abraham, Isaac and Jacob, and on to Israel as a nation (Gen. 47:27; Exod. 1:7). It is finally why, on the eve of their entry into the promised land, God told Israel he would bless them, multiply them, make them fruitful and enable them to fill the earth by subduing the nations around them (Deut. 7:13-16).

And notice another interesting phenomenon. Every time, from Noah to Jacob, that God spoke these words of command and promise, renewing the commission to Adam, these men responded by (1) pitching a tabernacle (2) on a mountain, (3) building an altar, (4) worshipping God, and (5) almost always calling the place the house of God. The combination of these five elements occurs elsewhere in the Old Testament only in the the building of the tabernacle of Moses and the temple of Solomon. What is happening? The patriarchs are reclaiming land by building worship areas in fulfillment of the original commission of Gen. 1:26-28 that their offspring are to spread out to subdue the world from the base of a divine sanctuary or temple.

CHAPTER FIVE

THE LAND PROMISE TO ABRAHAM

What we have said thus far sets the stage for God's covenant with Abraham. God had commissioned Adam to extend the land boundaries and he failed. Following the flood, Noah was likewise commissioned, and he too failed. Humanity fell under God's judgment at Babel and all the nations of the earth were consigned to the worship of false gods, with the exception of one man, Abraham, whom God picked out of his idolatrous culture and with whom he made a covenant. According to the genealogies of Genesis 5 and 11, there were ten generations from Adam to Noah, and ten from Noah to Abraham. Biblical genealogies are selective and the equality of the numbers is meant to make a point. As with Noah, Abraham initiates a new period in divine history. Once again, the commission to extend the land is about to be given. It is important to remember this, because the land promise to Abraham and his seed is *not something new, but rather a continuation* of God's intention to establish his kingdom rule through possessing the lands of the earth. That is to say, the land promise to Abraham and its eventual fulfillment through Moses and Joshua, cannot be seen outside the bigger picture of God's intention to restore Eden. *It is not an end in itself, but rather a stop along the way.*

From the beginning (Gen. 12:1-3), God promises to make Abraham a great nation, and clearly a nation cannot exist without either people or land. God promises Abraham both. In Gen. 15:1-6, in the face of Abraham's childlessness, God reaffirms his promise of a son, and that his descendants would be innumerable like the stars. He then tells Abraham that after a period of four hundred years, his offspring would inherit the land of Canaan (15:18). In Genesis 17, in spite of Abraham's disobedience in taking matters into his own hands (as recorded in chapter 16), God reaffirms and expands on his promise. Previously God had spoken of the possession of Canaan, but now he goes much further. Abraham is to be the "father of a multitude of nations" (17:5), to which he adds, "I will make you into nations, and kings shall come from you" (17:6). This is reinforced later, where God says "I will surely multiply your offspring as the stars of heaven and as the sand that is on the seashore. And your offspring shall possess the gate of his enemies, and in your offspring shall all the nations of the earth be blessed" (22:17-18). In other words, Abraham is to serve as father of a chosen community *by which God will bless all the nations of the world.* The promise cannot be seen in isolation. It stands clearly in the line of the previous commissions given to Adam and to Noah, both of whom were commanded to *fill the earth* with their descendants and extend the boundaries of God's rule. The end goal of God's plan goes far beyond Israel. Israel is the instrument by which God's kingdom is to reach the nations.

Dispensationalists argue that the land promise to Abraham is unconditional and therefore permanent. Regardless of how often the Jews disobeyed, even to the point of rejecting the Messiah, the land promise remains. But this is a simplistic view. From the beginning, fulfillment of the promise was not at all unconditional. It required obedience from Abraham. He himself made the choice to leave his home and head to Canaan. In spite of his disobedience which resulted in the birth of Ishmael, he determined to remain faithful to the Lord. Many years after Isaac was born, he made the choice to sacrifice him if that is what

God had required. In fact, all the promises of chapter 22 are conditional on Abraham's obedience: they will come to pass "because you have obeyed my voice" (22:18). In the final analysis, of course, the promise is an expression of God's grace. However, in chapter 15, Abraham arranges a sacrifice and God passes between the parts of the animal. Ancient near eastern tradition saw the one who passed between the pieces as committing himself to performing a vow. The ultimate fulfillment of God's promise rests with him, yet it does require human obedience to operate.

The land promise to Abraham was indeed fulfilled through Moses and Joshua, but then the land was lost at the exile. The ultimate goal of the land promise, to extend the boundaries of God's rule to the ends of the earth, never came to fruition. But how is this ever to happen when Abraham's descendants turn out not to have the faithfulness of Abraham? Even when Israel returned after the exile, they showed little inclination to obey God, and languished under a succession of foreign rulers. That is why both John the Baptist (Mt. 3:7-10) and Jesus (Jn. 8:39-47) told the Jews they were no children of Abraham at all. So if God has guaranteed fulfillment of the promise to Abraham that through Israel his kingdom rule would come to the nations, God must himself supply a descendant of Abraham who will walk with God in perfect obedience so that the promise is fulfilled. *That descendant is Christ.*

He is the one who will fulfill the promises of the covenant that the knowledge of God will come to the nations of the earth. He is the singular, not plural "offspring" to whom the promise comes (Gal. 3:16). And if the land promise is given to Abraham *and his seed* (singular), then the land promise, according to Gal. 3:16, is ultimately inherited *not by a physical nation* who proved disobedient to the point of rejecting God's Messiah, but by the only perfectly faithful descendant Abraham ever had, Christ himself. How exactly it can be said that the land promise is inherited by Christ we will show in the rest of this study.

The texts which speak of Abraham's "offspring" are informative. In Gen. 13:15; 17:7-8, God makes the promise to Abraham and his "offspring" or "seed." The word can be taken collectively, though Paul, as we've seen above, interprets it as referring to one individual, Christ. Yet Abraham's name change from Abram ("exalted father") to Abraham ("father of a multitude" (17:5) in the promise passage of chapter 17 indicates that his offspring will somehow include the nations of the earth: "Your name shall be Abraham, for I have made you the father of a multitude of nations… I will make you into nations, and kings shall come from you" (17:6). Gen. 22:17b clearly identifies the "offspring" as an individual who will "possess the gate of his enemies" and in whom "shall all the nations of the earth be blessed" (22:18). Putting these texts together shows us there is one perfect offspring who will then enable other offspring to inherit the land promise, which has now been extended to the nations of the earth. This points us back to the original commission to Adam, reiterated to Noah, to extend the land of the garden or kingdom to the ends of the earth.

The immediate expression of the land promise to Abraham, however, was contained within the borders of Canaan, the land spoken of in Gen 15:18-21, which extended from the river of Egypt to the river Euphrates. We should not be surprised at the incremental nature of the fulfillment of the land promise, for the expression of God's restoration of the land began in a small worship space to which Cain and Abel were invited, then was manifested at Bethel, where Jacob encountered the angels of God, and then was made permanent through the establishment of the tabernacle in the wilderness, where God's presence dwelt within the holy of holies. The possession of the land proceeds step by step. Following through Scripture carefully shows us how this promise develops, with setbacks along the way, but always pointing toward God's perfect plan, and how that plan itself is developed over time.

CHAPTER SIX

THE RISE AND FALL OF ISRAEL

Israel's entry into the promised land is pictured in terms which link it back to Eden. In the song which follows the passage through the Red Sea, Israel is pictured as a tree planted in a mountain sanctuary (Exod. 15:17), which according to Genesis 2 and Ezekiel 38 is a description of Eden. When Moses was born, his mother saw that he was "good" (Exod. 2:2), the same phrase used of God surveying the creation in Genesis 1. The birth of Moses and the exodus from Egypt initiated a new chapter in God's plan to restore the land under his kingship. In the Exodus, as at creation, God brings his people forth out of the waters of chaos. The continuity with Eden shows that the *land promise to Abraham is not to be seen in isolation or as en end it itself, but as part of a continuous plan of God to restore what was lost in the garden.*

Deuteronomy describes Israel at the end of the wilderness period and about to inherit the land. What it tells us about Israel and the land is significant.

First, the land promise has both conditional and unconditional elements. The land is a certainly a gift from God — the phrase "the land the Lord our God is giving us" occurs over thirty times in Deuteronomy as well as three times in Joshua. It is not something Israel either deserves or has earned. In that sense, it is an unconditional gift. On the other hand, ongoing possession of the land does include some conditions being met. Blessings were pronounced from Mount Gerizim, while curses were spoken from Mount Ebal (Deuteronomy 27). The first 14 verses of Deuteronomy 28 list the blessings of obedience, but by contrast the last 54 verses enumerate the consequences of disobedience, culminating in the prospect of a return to Egyptian bondage. That is to say, the duration of the promise is limited by the faithfulness of the people to whom the promise was given, the nation of Israel. It cannot be argued from Scripture that the land promise to Israel as a nation is permanent or completely unconditional without regard to obedience.

Second, the land is described in terms which recall Eden. It contains an Eden-like abundance of foliage, rich pastures, milk and honey. It offers extended lifespan without the illnesses of Egypt. This immediately connects the promised land with the mission of God in Eden to extend the boundaries of his kingdom. It is not an isolated moment in God's plan, but is integrally connected with his purposes throughout history. This point is further emphasized in Deuteronomy by seven references to multiplying and being multiplied in the land, reinforcing the mandate to Adam to be fruitful and multiply and thus to extend the boundaries of the land.

Third, Deuteronomy re-institutes the Edenic promise of a seventh-day rest, thus providing another link to the garden. In Eden, the creation of humanity is followed by God resting and taking up rulership of his creation through his image-bearers. The promised land is the place where God will give his people rest from their enemies (12:10), the concept of rest being linked with the seventh-day sabbath. As in Eden, the seventh day marks the rulership of God over creation exercised through his people. Surveying the Bible as a whole, this theme of rest both looks back to Eden and ahead to Christ. According to Heb. 4:1-11, the rest offered to God's people was fulfilled not in Israel's possession of the promised land, but in Christ. These points, which connect the possession of the promised land with both Eden and Christ are significant. They show us that the land promise fulfilled in Israel through Moses and Joshua must be seen as *a step on the way to something greater, rather than an end in itself.* We will come back to this concept later in terms of its fulfillment in the New Testament.

Fourth, Israel receives the land as an inheritance. Israel is depicted as God's son (Deut. 1:31; 8:5), the one to whom the father's inheritance comes (Deut. 4:20-21; 15:4). This is significant in light of Christ's identity as the ultimate Son, which thus identifies him equally as the true Israel and as the ultimate inheritor of the land promise.

From its beginning, Joshua describes the advancement of the Edenic mandate by the conquest of Canaan through its emphasis on taking possession of the ground: "Every place that the sole of your foot will tread upon I have given to you" (Josh. 1:3). When in chapter 18 Joshua set up the tent of meeting in Shiloh and all Israel gathers, it was a declaration that God had taken up his rest in the land and begun to rule (see also Josh. 11:23; 14:15). Yet even Joshua was unable to subdue the land entirely, and as history moved forward, Judges presents a mixed picture of victory and defeat, obedience and failure. Israel achieves rest, yet then loses it, as the various conflicts portrayed in Judges play out. In spite of the extraordinary set of events which led Israel to the promised land, the fulfillment of the command to extend God's territory requires something more.

The highpoint of Israel's history as a nation came during the reigns of David and Solomon. David's reign is pictured as a continuation of the Edenic mandate, for his rule gives his people the seventh day rest (2 Sam. 7:1, 10-11). The rest God promised through both Moses (Deut. 12:9-10) and the rest obtained under Joshua (Josh. 21:44; 22:4; 23:1) was inferior by comparison with that achieved under David, who subdued the violent enemies that had plagued Israel since the days of Joshua (2 Sam. 7:10), and who achieved victory over every foe. The land was secure. Not only this, David was a man of God under whose rule high spiritual standards were set in the nation, unlike the old days of idolatry. Yet the events of David's adultery and the subsequent tumult and rebellion in his family showed that all was not well.

David's legacy included the plans he laid for the building of the temple by his son Solomon. The temple was the first time a permanent visible manifestation of the dwelling place of God existed since Eden. It succeeded the tabernacle, which was temporary in nature. We have suggested that Eden was a garden temple. If this is the case, and if the Abrahamic mandate was to take up the Edenic mandate of pushing out the boundaries of the kingdom through taking hold of the land promise, then we would expect both the Mosaic tabernacle and Solomon's temple to have connections to the original garden temple. Consider the following: (1) When Adam failed in his duty as a priest and was expelled from the garden, two cherubim took over his priestly role; they "guarded" the way to the tree of life (Gen. 3:24). The same cherubim reappear guarding the ark of the covenant in the holy of holies. (2) The tree of life was probably the model for the lampstand placed directly outside the holy of holies. (3) The wood and stone carvings of gourds, flowers and pomegranates that gave the temple a garden-like appearance (1 Kgs. 6:18, 29, 32, 35; 7:18-20) point back to Eden. (4) The entrance to Eden was from the east, which was also the direction from which one entered both the tabernacle and the temple. (5) As mentioned earlier, the duties of the priests in the tabernacle are described using the same two Hebrew verbs (to guard and to keep) used to describe the duties of Adam in the garden.

The building of the temple was therefore a significant advance in the fulfilling of the Edenic mandate. The presence of God, once manifested in the garden, was now again permanently manifested in a physical place. The temple stood at the heart of the land, and signified a step in God's plan to restore Eden. Not only did Solomon extend the boundaries of Israel for the first time to the full extent of what had been promised to Abraham (1 Kgs. 4:24), Solomon's fame spread to all nations. Judah and Israel were, in Abrahamic terms, "as many as the sand by the sea," and his wisdom was described as like "sand on the seashore" (1 Kgs. 4:29). Solomon is contrasted to Adam in his desire to know wisdom in order to serve God (1 Kgs. 3:9), rather than seeking knowledge to make himself independent of God (Gen. 2:16-7; 3:1-7). The mentions of vines and fig trees (1 Kgs. 4:25) suggest the restoration of the garden. In his prayer, Solomon declares both that God has given his people rest and that not one word of all that was promised to Moses has failed (1 Kgs. 8:56). Under Solomon, the extension of Eden through the fulfillment of the Abrahamic mandate reached a new high.

Yet all was quickly lost. Following the dedication of the temple (1 Kings 8), Solomon turned away from the Lord (1 Kings 11) and incredibly, in the next 21 chapters, there are only two further references to the temple. Solomon's death is immediately followed by the rebellion of the northern tribes and the dividing of the nation. The glory was gone.

CHAPTER SEVEN

THE PROPHETS AND THE RESTORATION OF ISRAEL

This leads us to the prophets. Their consistent theme is the rebellion of Israel and its consequences, primarily the loss of the land. Yet at the same time they see into a future in which God restores both Israel and the land. Their writings will prove the key to our understanding of how both the Edenic mandate to extend the kingdom and the Abrahamic promise of the land is realized *not in the old physical Israel but instead under the prophesied Davidic kingdom restored through the coming of the Messiah.* Failure to understand the prophetic writings and how they are fulfilled in Christ will lead us, as it did the Jewish teachers of the law, to a completely mistaken understanding of the land promise.

The message of Isaiah is clear: Israel has come under judgment and will be expelled from the land. The expulsion is exactly what Moses had warned about in Deuteronomy: possession of the promised land was conditional upon obedience (Deut. 30:15-20). Only a remnant will be spared (Isa. 1:8-9). God's people will be exiled by a fierce and unmerciful enemy (Isa. 5:8-30). Jeremiah, in whose lifetime Judah fell, indicts the nation for breaking the covenant, and so they will come under the curse prophesied in Deuteronomy (Jer. 11:1-8). Ezekiel, writing from exile, describes both Israel and Judah as young girls rescued by the Lord who then turned to prostitution (Ezekiel chapters 16 and 23). As a result, the land is defiled (chapters 6-7), God has abandoned the temple (chapter 10) and his presence has departed (11:22-25). The penalty for disobedience is loss of the land. The gift God gave had been forfeited.

Yet judgment is transformed into hope. Ten of the sixteen writing prophets (Isaiah, Jeremiah, Ezekiel, Hosea, Joel, Amos, Obadiah, Micah, Zephaniah and Zechariah) speak of a future restoration of Israel. See for instance Isa. 40; Jer. 24:1-10; 29:10-14; Ezek. 36:8-15. The exile will turn out to be God's way of preserving a remnant (Isa. 1:9; 11:10-12, 16; 46:3-4; Jer. 23:1-4; 31:7-8; Joel

2:32; Mic. 2:12; 4:6-7; Zech. 8:11-13), and it is this remnant who will inherit the promises, not the nation as a whole. This gives us some perspective on Paul's understanding in Romans 9-11 of God's preservation of a faithful remnant (as opposed to the Jewish people as a whole) who will inherit the promises.

This return from exile comes in two stages. The first is historical, under Cyrus, who allows some Jews to return (Isa. 44:24-45:1; Ezra 1:1-3). But this was only a partial restoration, and the Jews who did return were never able to re-establish their own nation, neither did they seek a restoration of Biblical obedience. Haggai 1 and Malachi 1-2 show the sad spiritual state of the exiles who did return. But the prophets spoke of a greater return from exile which would produce a far different result. What is this greater restoration of which they spoke?

Isaiah begins by speaking of the events of the "latter days," when the house of the Lord turns into a mountain, in fact the highest mountain of the earth. Not only Israel, but all the nations of the earth, will come to this latter-day temple-mountain, and all nations will come under the rule of God (Isa. 2:1-4). When we consider that Ezekiel portrays Eden as a garden-mountain (Ezek. 28:13-14), we realize Isaiah is foreseeing the restoration of Eden. At that time, the "branch" of the Lord, a clearly

Messianic figure, will cleanse the faithful remnant, and over Jerusalem the cosmic sign of the Mosaic cloud by day and fire by night will reappear (Isaiah 5). Isaiah ends in the portrayal of an Eden-like garden on a holy mountain called both a new heavens and earth and also a renewed Jerusalem (65:17-22). This land is called Zion and will be "born in one day" (66:8), and to it will come the glory of the nations (66:12), thus fulfilling the Abrahamic promise that in his seed will all the nations of the earth be blessed. A time is coming when God will gather "all nations and tongues" (66:18).

But in between the initial return and these clearly eschatological events, something else is prophesied: the Spirit will be outpoured on the descendants of Israel such that even Gentiles will call on the name of the Lord (Isa. 44:1-5). This astonishing event will be performed by the Servant of the Lord, whose mission is twofold: to restore the saved among Israel and to be a light to the nations that God's salvation may reach to the ends of the earth (49:1-6). Here we see clearly both the Edenic mandate and the Abrahamic promise fulfilled. The rule of God will in some sense extend to the ends of the earth. This Servant is described as the Prince of Peace, the Mighty God and the Everlasting Father who will restore the throne of David (11:6-7). He will be called Immanuel, born of a virgin (7:14). The Servant will fulfill the commission given to Adam, Noah and Israel. He will succeed where all before him have failed. Those he calls will come from the four corners of the earth (49:12). Some form of restoration of Eden will occur: "For the Lord comforts Zion; he comforts all her waste places and makes her wilderness like Eden, her desert like the garden of the Lord" (51:3). An undoubted reference to a worldwide restoration of Eden occurs at 27:6: "In days to come, Jacob shall take root, Israel shall blossom and put forth shoots and fill the whole world with fruit."

Isaiah continues on this theme of restoration. The ransomed of the Lord shall return in a new Exodus (51:11). The reign of God will come (52:7). The Lord will redeem Jerusalem, and salvation will come to the nations of the earth (52:9-10). All this will come through the Servant, the man of sorrows wounded for our transgressions, cut off from the land of the living, yet who will see his offspring and be satisfied (52:13-53:12). His substitutionary atonement will initiate a new covenant (55:3) for the peoples and nations of the world (55:4-5). The Gentiles also will become the servants of the Lord, brought to his holy mountain, where his house "shall be called a house of prayer for all peoples" (56:7). The remnant of Israel will be joined by the saved of the Gentiles (56:8).

So Isaiah clearly portrays the idea that the restoration of the land and the fulfillment of the promise to Abraham comes through the atoning work of the prophesied Suffering Servant. This restoration seems to occur within history, *but is also interpreted eschatologically,* as if to suggest a *two stage fulfillment* of the land promise. First he says clearly: "He who takes refuge in me shall possess the land and shall inherit my holy mountain" (Isa. 57:13). But then, the picture of a renewed world is painted for us in chapter 60. In this world, foreshadowing John's vision in the Bible's last two chapters, neither sun nor moon is needed, for God is an everlasting light. Here Isaiah speaks of God's people *possessing the land forever* (60:21). The land inherited is not the earthly promised land, but something far different and greater, linked to the new creation of Rev. 21-22. In chapter 61, the Messianic prophecy quoted by Jesus in the synagogue of Nazareth and applied to himself in his earthly ministry, speaks of God's people being called the priests of the Lord, and "*in their land* they shall possess a double portion" (Isa. 61:7). So there is a counterpoint, in which the land promised to Abraham is referred to as possessed both within the context of history but only through the work of the Messiah, yet also seen as an eternal reality. Rev. 1:6; 5:10 understand the promise of priesthood given through Moses to Israel in Exodus 19 as in fact inherited by the church. All this means that inheritance of the land is connected with the coming of Christ, and linked in some manner with the church.

This makes sense in light of Isaiah's understanding that possession of the land comes about only through the atoning work of the Messiah. Isaiah prophesies a time beyond the exile when God will bring forth a faithful remnant who will be "possessors of my mountains" (65:9). Yet again the promise flows from history into eternity: this last-days land involves a new heavens and a new earth (65:17; 66:22), thus tying it again to the new creation of Revelation 21-22 (and not, it needs to be noted, to a supposed earthly millennium). It also involves a new Jerusalem (65:18-19) and a holy mountain (65:25), both clearly geographical references. This can only refer to the ultimate fulfillment of the Abrahamic promise. God's people will receive a new name, as in the promise to Christians in Rev. 2:12; 22:4, and will receive blessing in the land (65:15-16).

The other prophets bear witness to Isaiah's vision. Jeremiah, like Isaiah, sees a new exodus besides which the original exodus will pale into insignificance (Jer. 16:14-15). This exodus will include people of all nations who seek the Lord (12:14-17). A future repentance of Israel will result in all nations coming to know the Lord and glory in him (4:1-2). A Davidic king will arise to restore the people and bring them back to the land (Jeremiah 30). This event will occur in the "latter days" (30:24). This inheritance of the land promise is clearly not a reference to return from the Babylonian exile, for it is an exodus worldwide in nature (31:8), involving all peoples, not just Jews. In those days God will make a new covenant with his people, not the covenant they broke when they came out of Egypt (31:31-32). His law will be written on their hearts (31:33), a passage Hebrews 8 understands as a reference to the new covenant in Christ. This links the fulfillment of the land promise with Christ, just as in Isaiah. But Jeremiah goes further. This inheritance of the land promise will involve Jerusalem being rebuilt, never to be overthrown again (31:38-40). God will make an everlasting covenant with his people (32:40), who will be cleansed from sin (33:8), and the city of Jerusalem will be a joy, praise and glory to God before all the nations of the earth (33:9). There can be no doubt fulfillment of the Abrahamic promise is referred to. All this will be accomplished through a righteous branch from the house of David (33:14; see Isa. 11:1-10). Jerusalem will be given a new name, "The Lord is our righteousness" (33:16). David's descendant will initiate an eternal rule (33:17). The new covenant people will be as numerous as the sands of the sea (33:22), thus fulfilling the Edenic mandate and the Abrahamic promise. Once again, as in Isaiah, the fulfillment of the land promise comes in two stages. The first is through the earthly work of the Messiah. It entails a new covenant initiated through the Messiah and including the Gentiles. The second is eternal in nature.

We find similar themes in Ezekiel. Ezekiel speaks of God's judgment on Israel (16:1-43), who has shown herself even more corrupt than the surrounding pagan nations (16:44-52). Yet a restoration is coming both for Israel and these nations (16:53-58). The Lord is going to establish an everlasting covenant with Israel (16:59-60), and in that day he will give these nations to Israel not as the unfaithful sisters they were, but instead as daughters, "but not on account of the covenant with you" (16:61). A new covenant people will be constituted not on the basis of race, but on the basis of faithfulness to the Lord. While God's sanctuary had been with the exiles in Babylon "for a while" (14:16), he is going to make a new covenant with his people that will deal with their sin (36:16-38), and as a result his sanctuary will be "in their midst forever" (37:26-28). The restoration of the sanctuary can only be seen as an expression of the fulfillment of the land promise, though how this prophetic vision is worked out and what this "sanctuary" will amount to, will not be made clear until its fulfillment. This restoration will include other nations. This new people will be one flock under the leadership of a new David (34:23-24).

The new covenant God will make is described in Edenic terms as a restored and lush environment from which fear and hunger are banished (34:25-31; also 36:8-15, 29-30). This new covenant will bring God's people *into their own land* (36:24), and will be marked by the infilling of the Spirit and forgiveness (36:25-29). The fulfillment of the land promise here is linked with the prophesied outpouring of the Holy Spirit at Pentecost. The chapter builds to a climax by saying *this restored land* will be "like the garden of Eden" (36:35).

In summary, Ezekiel prophesies a coming Davidic Messiah who will restore Israel, along with the faithful of pagan nations, through the outpouring of the Holy Spirit and the forgiveness of sin, *to a restored promised land which resembles the garden of Eden.* This is clearly not fulfilled in the historical return from Babylon, and neither is it fulfilled in the establishment of the political state of Israel in modern times. What is critical here is the connection of the Davidic Messiah with (1) the outpouring of the Spirit, (2) the forgiveness of sins, (3) the joining of faithful Jews and Gentiles together in (4) a new covenant, all of which is (5) linked with the fulfillment of the land promise. *Thus the land promise becomes inextricably tied to the new covenant and the church, not the old covenant and the nation of Israel or even the Jewish people.* Ezekiel prophesies a fulfillment of the land promise within history which is clearly linked to the church. How the church can represent a legitimate fulfillment of the land promise must be seen, as we will see, within the framework of the New Testament's statements concerning the extending of the kingdom to the nations of the world.

This last-days filling of the Spirit is described at length in Ezekiel's picture of the valley of dry bones (chapter 37). When Jesus talked about being born again of the Spirit, he was referring to this passage, which was why in John 3 he rebuked Nicodemus, the teacher of Israel, for his inability to understand the reference. In this passage, the endowment of the Spirit upon God's new covenant people is again linked with the fulfillment of the land promise. First God says, "I will bring you into the land of Israel" (37:12), then he says, "I will put my Spirit within you, and you shall live, and I will place you in your own land" (37:14). Clearly, the prophet is speaking of a latter days fulfillment of the land of Israel which he ties to the coming of the Spirit, which of course is fulfilled at Pentecost. This is why Jesus puts such an importance on understanding this passage correctly. This Israel is not a piece of middle eastern geography, but refers to something much greater. The new covenant will involve a latter-days exodus in which God brings his people as one nation into the land, "on the mountains of Israel"

(37:22). God's sanctuary, lost in Eden, is to be restored on an everlasting basis which impacts the nations of the world (37:26-28). Israel is to expand to fill the earth through the coming of the Messiah and the outpouring of the Spirit. Thus the land promise receives an initial fulfillment within history through the church, even though this does not exhaust the meaning of its final fulfillment in the new Jerusalem.

The latter comes into focus with the picture of the ideal end-times temple Ezekiel describes in chapters 40-48, a passage unparalleled in the Old Testament. To describe what he is saying, Ezekiel, like the other prophets, works with the material in front of him (in this case, a physical temple), much like John in Revelation 19 uses the imagery of the Messianic rider coming on a white horse, rather than describing him as driving a tank or piloting the latest generation of fighter aircraft. He is telling us that a new temple is coming, completely unlike the old, and it is linked with all the realities he has been speaking of in the previous chapters — the Davidic Messiah, the Spirit, the forgiveness of sins, the inclusion of the Gentiles, the restoration of Eden and so on. G.K. Beale, in his *Commentary on Revelation*, makes a convincing case that John took Ezekiel's vision of the temple, the city and the land, and saw it fulfilled in his vision of the eternal temple-city-land (parallels include the names of both cities, the shape of the cities, the presence of God in the cities, a renewed priesthood, the river of life and so on). The fact that Ezekiel is describing a city in prophetic or idealized, rather than literal terms is clear particularly in chapter 47, where an ever-deepening river flows from the temple throughout the land bringing cleansing and life to the dead places. The idea of the river is borrowed from the four rivers of the garden (four being the number of the whole earth), hence the presence of the tree of life in both visions. Both Ezekiel and John are portraying the ultimate fulfillment of the Edenic mandate *and the land promise* in the new Jerusalem, which is the eternal restoration of Eden, expanded to encompass the entire cosmos.

Centuries later, near the end of the age of the prophets, Zechariah picks up Isaiah's prophecy of the servant of the Lord, the righteous branch (3:8), who will remove the sin of his people "in a single day" (3:9) and restore Edenic type conditions (3:10). Later, he speaks of a king, "humble and mounted on a donkey, on a colt, the foal of a donkey," (9:9) who will bring an end to warfare and speak peace to the nations. The rule of this Messianic king (here the prophet quotes Psalm 72) shall be "from sea to sea, and from the River to the ends of the earth" (9:10). The blood of his covenant will set the prisoners free (9:11). It is significant that Zechariah quotes from

Psalm 72. The Psalm, written from the perspective of Solomon, speaks of a coming Messianic ruler whom Solomon would certainly have understood to come from the Davidic line, and who will restore Edenic conditions to earth as long as the sun and moon exist (verses 5-8). His dominion will be "from sea to sea, and from the River [the Euphrates] to the ends of the earth" (verse 8). This is a restatement of Exod. 23:31, where God promises the Israelites that their border shall be from the Euphrates to the Mediterranean and the Red Sea, a promise fulfilled in Solomon's own rule. Yet Solomon himself in this Psalm prophesies a new Davidic king whose rule will extend beyond the frontiers of geographical Israel to the very ends of the earth, and who will bring about a restoration of Eden, thus fulfilling the intention of God since his creation of humanity to extend his kingdom to the ends of the earth. All nations, not just Israel, will serve this king (verse 11). There is a further description of Eden-like conditions (verse 16), followed by this statement: "May people be blessed in him, all nations call him blessed!" (verse 17). This surely is phrased deliberately by Solomon to describe the fulfillment of the promise to Abraham that in his seed (the Messiah) all the nations of the world would be blessed. Solomon himself, through whom the land promise to Abraham was most convincingly, albeit temporarily, fulfilled, sees that what is represented by the land he rules is far from the ultimate fulfillment of the promise. How then could it be thought that a restored middle eastern Israel, with boundaries less than those under Solomon's rule, could represent that fulfillment?

The end of Old Testament revelation thus leaves us with the promise of a coming king who will both fulfill the promise to Abraham regarding the Messianic blessing on the nations of the earth, and the Messianic completion of the mandate to restore Eden. The land promise is not only for Israel, and in fact extends far beyond Israel. This should not surprise us, for God's purpose from the beginning has been worldwide in nature. He is not interested in possession of a small piece of real estate in the middle east. He wants the entire cosmos. *And his possession of the cosmos is to be conceived in Hebraic, not Greek immaterial terms:* the renewed cosmos has both continuity and discontinuity with the present creation, in the way that Paul expresses regarding the relationship of the physical body of the present, fallen world and the renewed body of the eternal new creation in 1 Corinthians 15. The possession of the promised land under Moses turns out to be only an initial fulfillment. It was in fact lost through Israel's disobedience. The frustration of his purposes that came about when first Adam failed, then Noah, then Israel, is not the last word. His plan will be fulfilled through God's Messiah and his people.

PART THREE

THE LAND PROMISE IN THE NEW TESTAMENT

CHAPTER EIGHT

THE LAND PROMISE IN MATTHEW

And so we come to the New Testament. The mission of Christ, from the very beginning, was the proclamation of the kingdom of God — the kingdom has arrived, albeit not in its consummate, eschatological form. The kingdom mandate is the fulfillment of the Abrahamic promise, for Jesus will not return until the kingdom has extended to every people group on earth (Mk. 13:10; Matt. 24:14). The New Testament does not speak much of land in a literal sense, for the same reason that Jesus did not link his ministry to the physical temple or to the physical city of Jerusalem. His kingdom is empowered by the Holy Spirit indwelling his followers, not represented by an earthly ruler sitting on a throne in Jerusalem. In the Old Testament, God makes a place, then creates a people to live in it. In the New Testament, God makes a people, then creates the place for them to live. The kingdom is fulfilled in two stages: first on earth in a spiritual form, then in the new creation in a literal, physical and geographical form, albeit transcending the scope of our current cosmos.

The new creation pictured in the last two chapters of the Bible is the ultimate fulfillment of the land promise to Abraham. It represents the triumph of Christ in extending the boundaries of the kingdom where Adam, Noah and Israel had failed. The promise is literally, and not merely spiritually fulfilled, in that the New Testament presents the new creation as a physical reality, unlike pagan concepts of the immaterial afterworld. This new cosmos is related to the old as the resurrection body is to the physical body. It is both a recreation and a renewal. Believers now live in the present reality of a kingdom which has invaded this world, but live also in anticipation of its future fulfillment. That is why the New Testament is not interested in the idea of a land in the order of the old covenant land, but rather looks forward to its eschatological fulfillment in the new creation, which represents the final link in a chain which commences in the garden and concludes in the new Jerusalem.

The land promise to Abraham is a step on the way, but not the final destination. *To see the fulfillment of the land promise in the form of a nation largely composed of non-believers in a geographical place in the middle east is to separate that promise entirely from the work of Christ and thus to diminish it completely.* It commits the dispensational error of seeing Christ as only one goal of God's plan in history, Israel being the other. In the dispensational scheme, Christ is no longer all and in all, he is merely one dimension of God's solution for humanity. This must surely be seen as false teaching and a fundamental denial of the gospel, even if its proponents in all sincerity do not see it that way.

At the beginning of the New Testament, Matthew commences his gospel with these words: "(The) book of the genealogy of Jesus Christ" (Matt. 1:1). The Greek phrase is *biblos geneseos,* meaning literally the book of Genesis or "the book of the genesis" (birth). The words are drawn from the only two places they appear in the Old Testament, Gen. 2:4 and 5:1. The first text refers to the original creation of humanity, the second to the renewed creation through Noah after the flood. The point Matthew is making is that Christ represents a fulfillment of God's promises in the creation of humanity — a new creation is being inaugurated. In this case, we would expect that with the new creation would come a new land. Land to be possessed came with the first creation, and land to be possessed came after the flood. And of course, land to be possessed came with the promise to Abraham.

As Matthew presents the genealogy of Christ in the succeeding verses, he fashions the ancestry of Christ into three sets of fourteen generations. An astute reader of the Bible will notice that he picks and chooses, for the list hardly begins to cover all of Jesus' ancestors. The number 42 is significant, in that it represents six sets of seven. It thus points to a fulfillment through Christ of the seventh set of seven, as in the Jubilee, the time of forgiveness of debts. Further, in placing Abraham at the head of the first set of generations and David at the head of the second set, it acknowledges Christ as the fulfillment of both Abraham, to whom the promise of international blessing was given, and David, whom the Old Testament sees as the great ruler of Israel and the the one from whom the Messiah will come. So Christ is the fulfillment of the promise to Abraham that in his seed all nations would be blessed, and he is also the fulfillment of the promise of a great Davidic king who would establish the kingdom in a way even David was unable to do. But Matthew adds a third set of fourteen generations, which focusses on the exile. Thus Jesus is also seen as the one who will truly deliver the people from exile and bring them into a renewed Israel, and who will save them from the results of their sin. And at the conclusion of the genealogy, this is exactly what Matthew says: Jesus is the one who will "save his people from their sins" (Matt. 1:21).

Matthew's goal is thus to present Jesus as the one who will fulfill the promises of land and worldwide blessing given to Abraham; as the one who will be the prophesied king who will possess and restore David's kingdom in an unimaginably escalated way; *and as the one who will bring his people back to their land from exile.*

If this is true, then Matthew's quotation of Hos. 11:1 is significant: "Out of Egypt I called my son" (Matt. 2:15). Hosea makes the statement in reference to the original exodus, but then goes on to prophesy both the exile and a new exodus, this time out of Assyria. Hosea uses the word "son" to refer to Israel, but would surely have been aware of the Messianic prophecies of the Old Testament concerning the son of David who would restore the Davidic kingdom in a way that, in the end, was unfulfilled by the return from exile. Matthew now uses Hosea's language to declare that a new exodus has in fact begun, this time led not by Moses but by the prophesied son of David, Jesus Christ. The holy family's return from Egypt marks a renewed, indeed the true fulfillment of

Hosea's prophecy. Matthew sees the ministry of Jesus as the prophesied restoration of the land, for reclamation of the land is surely the purpose of a Biblical exodus. *If there is a new exodus, there must be a new land.* In quoting Hosea and applying the theme of a new exodus to Jesus, Matthew redefines the meaning of the land promise. Jesus did not come as a political Messiah to take back the land from the Romans. *The land promise instead reaches its initial, earthly fulfillment in Jesus' proclamation that the kingdom of God has arrived.* The land promise thus begins its fulfillment in a way deeper than the limited insight of the prophets, but absolutely true to the story line of the Bible, which is the extension of the kingdom from its beginnings in the tabernacle and then the land of Israel to its ultimate fulfillment first in the earthly spread of the gospel to every nation, and consummately in the new Jerusalem.

In the Sermon on the Mount, Jesus makes the statement, "Blessed are the meek, for they shall inherit the earth" (Matt. 5:5). Here Jesus is quoting Ps. 37:11, "But the meek shall inherit the land." The word "land" in the Psalm is *eretz*, the Hebrew word used in the phrase *eretz Yisrael*, the land of Israel. The Psalm is eschatological in nature, meaning that it speaks of a time in the distant future in which, among other things, the meek shall inherit the land (see verses 18, 29, 34). The word inherit in Hebrew *(yarash)* is frequently used of Israel inheriting the promised land. Here Jesus takes the land promise and interprets it in light of both the eschatological intent of the Psalm and of his own proclamation of the kingdom of God. He is saying that it is those who follow him who will inherit the Promised Land, *eretz Yisrael*. In making this statement concerning the land, he universalizes it: *it is no longer the land of Israel which is to be inherited, it's the entire earth.* Thus Jesus radically reinterprets the land promise in light of its initial fulfillment in his own ministry.

In Matt. 11:28, Jesus extends an offer to those who would follow him: "Come to me, all who labor and are heavy laden, and I will give you rest." We touched on the theme of rest earlier in our examination of the Old Testament, and here we explore it more fully in its Biblical context in both Testaments. The word "rest" is heavily laden with Biblical meaning. The verb used to describe how God "put" Adam into the garden (Gen. 2:15) is the word usually translated as "rest," so that the best translation would be "God put Adam into the Garden to rest." Yet Genesis clearly says that God put Adam into the garden to work it and keep it (Gen. 2:15). Adam exercised the government of God over the garden, yet this activity of ruling and reigning is described as rest! Adam lost this place of governing when he disobeyed

God and was ejected from his place of rest. So it's not surprising that Israel's inheriting the land is described as God's giving them rest (Deut. 12:8-10). The rest and the reign of God's people in extending his kingdom which was lost in the garden is to be taken up again as Israel enters the Promised Land. Now, coming back to the Gospel account, Jesus is telling his followers that the rest promised first in the garden, then in the Promised Land, finds it true fulfillment in him.

There is another important point to be made about this concept of rest. There are many links between the garden, the tabernacle and the temple, principally around the concept of priests in a garden temple, which explains the presence not only of the cherubim but also of the garden-like carvings and artwork. But there is another fascinating connection. When we examine Scripture, we find that the building of the tabernacle under Moses, and later the building of the temple under Solomon, were both patterned on God's creation of the universe. Seven times from Gen. 1:3 through 1:26, the phrase "And God said" occurs, each of which marks a stage of the creation process. At the end of the sixth day, it says that "God saw everything that he had made, and behold, it was very good" (Gen. 1:31). After this, God rested (Gen. 2:1). The building of the tabernacle was likewise fashioned around seven creative words of God,

"And the Lord said" (Exod. 25:1; 30:11, 17, 22, 34; 31:1, 12). At the end of the tabernacle creation process, it says, "Moses saw all the work" the people had done according to the command of the Lord, and he blessed them for it (Exod. 39:43). Then when the tabernacle was finished, God's presence entered into it and his glory filled it so that Moses was not able to enter (Exod. 40:34-35).

What was happening in this process? God was taking up his rest. As it was in the garden, so it is in the tabernacle. This becomes even clearer as we look to the building of the temple. Here we find — and it cannot be a coincidence — that Solomon took seven years to build it (1 Kgs. 6:38), that he dedicated it on the seventh month during the feast of booths, which lasted seven days (1 Kings 8), and that his speech of dedication was built around seven prayers (1 Kgs. 8:31-55). And then — and this is the critical point — just as God rested on the seventh day from his work of creation, so when the temple was finished, God once again took up a resting place. How do we know this? The psalmist tells us: "Arise, O Lord, and go to your *resting place,* you and the ark of your might... For the Lord has chosen Zion; he has desired it for his dwelling place. This is my *resting place* forever; here I will dwell, for I have desired it" (Ps. 132:8, 13-14).

The idea of rest under God's rule is therefore associated with the garden, with Israel entering the promised land, and with both the tabernacle and the temple. In each case, the idea of entering rest is equated with possessing the land, whether that of the garden or the Promised Land. Yet on each occasion, the rest was forfeited. *Jesus now offers his followers the rest lost through disobedience.* Hebrews 4 enlarges on this, telling us that God has prepared a rest for his people, and that for the first time through Christ we can enter it. God only rests in order to rule over a land. This means that the land promise that runs from Adam to Solomon is fulfilled not in a piece of geographical territory but in Christ's kingdom, first spiritually on earth and consummately physically in the new Jerusalem.

When Jesus ascended and sat down at the right hand of God, he began his rule, just as God the Father had done in the garden, the tabernacle and the temple. That is why it was as he was about to ascend to the Father and take his seat at God's right hand, he spoke words which were surely a deliberate repetition of the commands to Adam, Noah and Abraham to be fruitful and multiply and thus extend the boundaries of God's land: "All authority in heaven and on earth has been given to me. Go therefore and make disciples of *all nations*..." (Matt. 28:18).

CHAPTER NINE

THE LAND PROMISE IN HEBREWS AND PAUL

This theme of rest and inheriting the land reappears in Hebrews. Heb. 4:10 goes back to the rest of Genesis 2 and connects it with the rest through inheritance of the land offered in Deut. 12:8-10. The author, alluding to Numbers 14, points out that the wilderness generation failed to enter that rest through their disobedience. And ultimately, as he and every Jew understood, the rest offered through possession of the land was lost at the exile and never truly regained. But the promise of entering the rest remains (Heb. 4:1), and is possessed not by a latter-days recreated state of Israel consisting largely of those who reject Christ, but rather by all those who do believe in Christ: "For we who have believed enter that rest" (Heb. 4:3). The author quotes the Psalmist, speaking in Ps. 95:7-11, as urging the people that "today" they can enter the rest that the wilderness generation failed to enter. Hebrews draws from this the conclusion that there must be a further rest beyond that promised to the children of Israel represented by the literal promised land.

The writer knows that some did enter that literal rest, yet he sees the Psalmist as pointing to a rest beyond this which still needs to be entered into. This he interprets as being the rest which is found in Christ. The rest of the promised land is therefore a type, a prophetic foreshadowing, of the rest in Christ. The reason this makes good exegetical sense for the author is that he is following the concept of rest from the garden through the land and the temple to Christ. The land of Canaan is only a stop along the way to the true destination. But the rest always represents a tangible possession of territory where God rules; it is not merely a non-material reality which fails to operate powerfully in the world. That is why the rest in Christ involves the extension of the kingdom to the nations of the earth through the power of the Holy Spirit and involving changed lives, families and communities. This is a tangible, physical reality. It is also why the rest in Christ must find its ultimate fulfillment in a tangible territorial reality, which is portrayed for us in the Bible's last book. This is also confirmed in Hebrews 11, where the narrative moves from Abraham's tent in the promised land to the thought of being exiles on the earth seeking a homeland, not the land they had lived in, but a better, heavenly country (vv. 9-16). This heavenly country has received an initial fulfillment in Christ and those who (in Paul's words) are children of the "Jerusalem above" (Gal. 4:26). But the ultimate fulfillment of the rest and of the land will occur at the shaking of all things and the resulting unshakeable eternal kingdom (12:22-29). This is God's rest, God's promised land. The road to it runs not through geographical Israel, described by Paul as the "present Jerusalem" which is "in slavery with her children" (Gal. 4:25), but through Christ and his kingdom.

Paul amplifies on these themes in various places. Gen. 12:7 records God's promise to Abraham, "To your offspring I will give this land." This is the original statement of the land promise to Israel, hence a very significant verse. In Gal. 3:16, alluding to this text, Paul defines the "offspring" or "seed" referred to in the text as Christ. He also references this verse in Rom. 4:13, "The promise to Abraham and his offspring that he would be heir *of the world* did not come through the law but through the righteousness of faith." Here Paul makes a significant change in the wording of the Genesis text, to the effect that Abraham's offspring (Christ) would inherit not the "land" but the "world." This is a legitimate interpretation of Genesis in that the

Genesis text also says that in Abraham's seed *all the families of the earth* would be blessed (Gen. 12:3), a theme that is repeated in Gen. 22:18, "And in your offspring shall *all the nations of the earth* be blessed." To reinforce his point, Paul adds the comment in Rom. 4:16 that Abraham is "the father of us all," Jew and Gentile alike, citing Gen. 17:5, "I have made you the father *of many nations*" (Rom. 4:17). It is clear, therefore, that Paul regarded the land promise to Abraham as being fulfilled ultimately not in Israel's possession of Canaan, but rather in Abraham's offspring Christ, and the consequent Gospel expansion of the kingdom of God to every nation. Paul was no doubt also thinking of Jesus' statement in the Sermon on the Mount (alluded to above) that his followers would inherit not just the land but the whole earth. While the initial fulfillment of the land promise is through Christ and his kingdom spreading on earth, the consummate fulfillment of the land promise through Christ is in the renewed heavens and earth. This safeguards the literal or physical aspect of the land promise. It is fulfilled in Christ not merely in a real but spiritual sense in this age, in which the kingdom spreads to the nations, but also eschatologically in the renewal of the present creation.

Paul himself speaks of this in Rom. 8:18-25, where not only believers, but the creation itself will be set free from its present bondage into the glorious liberty of the children of God. First he tells us that God has adopted us in Christ as his children, and thus "heirs of God and fellow heirs with Christ" (Rom. 8:17). So when the offspring of Abraham (Christ) inherits the world and thus the Abrahamic land promise, so in Christ we as offspring of Abraham also inherit this promise (Rom. 4:13). Thus the land promise given to Abraham is fulfilled initially in the work of Christ, as the kingdom of God spreads to the nations of the world, and ultimately in the new creation. It is no accident that Paul's thinking moves seamlessly in the following verses of Romans 8 (starting at verse 18) from the idea of believers inheriting the world through Christ, in the initial fulfillment of the land promise, to the idea of the setting free of the creation as a whole, in the ultimate fulfillment of the land promise. Paul is surely on solid ground interpreting the land promise as a reality inherited by believers in Christ, for the land promise to Abraham, as we have seen, suggests the idea of its inheritance by the nations of the earth.

The concept of Christian believers inheriting the kingdom can also be found in Paul explicitly in 1 Cor. 15:50-58, and by direct implication in 1 Cor. 6:9-10 and Gal. 5:21, where the fact that the unrighteous will not inherit the kingdom presupposes that the righteous will inherit it. The original land promise, which itself represents a step in the restoration of Eden, is in Christ expanded, as per God's promise to Abraham, in light of Christ's preaching of the kingdom, to encompass the whole world as the gospel reaches every nation, a world which is then eschatologically renewed at Christ's return, at which point Eden is completely restored and the garden-temple expands to fill the whole cosmos.

CHAPTER TEN

THE LAND PROMISE IN REVELATION

In Rev. 1:1-3, John has reinterpreted significant passages from Dan. 2:28-29, 45, which prophesy a coming kingdom, and applied them to the church. The prophesied kingdom will vanquish all earthly kingdoms and bring God's rule to the earth. In verses 5b-6, this thought is reinforced. John gives praise to Christ: "To him who loves us and has freed us from our sins by his blood and made us a kingdom, priests to his God and Father, to him be glory and dominion forever and ever. Amen." This is a direct reference to Exod. 19:6: "You shall be to me a kingdom of priests and a holy nation." Notice how significant is the change of tense. What was prophesied as future in Exodus and applied to the people of Israel is now stated as an accomplished fact by John (the verb "made" is in the past tense) and applied to the church. "Kingdom" can mean kingship, royal power, or the exercise of that power. Believers do not merely live within a kingdom, as if the kingdom referred only to a geographical location. They exercise its kingly power, or perhaps more accurately, Christ exercises his kingly power through them. Put another way, the church is the place where or through which the kingdom power of God operates. God has chosen to exercise his kingly rule through his people. The prophesied latter-day kingdom of Daniel has arrived in Christ. The kingdom is the rule of God which now, through the church, will be extended to the ends of the earth and encompass every nation or people group before Jesus returns (Mk. 13:10; Matt. 24:14). The Exodus passage is quoted again in 5:10, where in the heavenly vision the elders praise the Lamb for making his people "from every tribe and language and people and nation" a "kingdom and priests to our God."

The story line of the Bible begins and ends in a garden temple. The land lost in Eden is reclaimed in the new Jerusalem. The first two chapters of the Bible and the last two chapters serve as remarkable bookends to everything in between. The river, the tree of life, the precious stones and the presence of God which marked the first garden-temple are all there in the second. The only difference is that the presence of evil is banished. The people of every "tribe and language and people and nation" ransomed by the Lamb (Rev. 5:9) represent first, the culmination of the command to be fruitful and multiply; second, the fulfillment of the promise to Abraham that his descendants would possess the nations; and third, the result of the great commission to make disciples of all nations. Revelation 21-22 collapses Ezekiel's vision of the temple, city and land into one city-garden-temple which has expanded to fill the creation. As G.K. Beale puts it: "The original Eden, Israel's old temple, old land and old city, never reached the universal goal for which they were designed. As such, they became imperfect typological realities pointing forward to a time when these would again become eschatological realities, whose design would reach their final goal" (*New Testament Biblical Theology*, p. 759).

Contrary to modern dispensationalism, orthodox Christian theology over the ages has held that the fulfillment of all Biblical prophecy is in Christ: "For all the promises of God find their Yes in him" (2 Cor. 1:20). The charge is frequently levelled by dispensationalists that proponents of orthodox or covenant theology view the church as replacing Israel and devaluing the promises to Abraham. This charge is untrue, because no one strictly advocates for the church as the fulfillment of Israel, but rather for Christ as the fulfillment of Israel, in fact for

Christ as the true Israel himself. He is the seed of the woman prophesied in Genesis, he is the seed of Abraham in whom the promise to Abraham is fulfilled. He is the son of David and inheritor of the restored Davidic kingdom. Those who are in Christ, whether Jew or Gentile, inherit the promises solely by virtue of their relationship with him.

Although the New Testament does not formally suggest that the land promise has been inherited by the church, it does make statements which point strongly in that direction. Beale says this: "Nevertheless, the NT does affirm that Christ has begun to fulfill the end-time prophecies of the expected 'Israel,' 'Jerusalem,' 'Zion,' 'temple,' and 'throne of David,' all of which were to be significant pieces of real estate in the coming new land of Israel. In that these prophecies pertained to significant parts of Israel's future landscape, Christ's beginning fulfillment of them in some way is an initial realization of part of the land promises" (Beale, *New Testament Biblical Theology*, p. 770). In one sense, Christ has begun a literal fulfillment of these promises by being physically raised from the dead. The OT prophets foresaw a literal kingdom ruled over by spiritually by a Messianic king, assuming that all these elements of a renewed Israel, land, kingdom and temple would be fulfilled at once. The NT reveals that these prophecies are fulfilled in two stages. This is what theologians call the "already-not yet" dynamic of this present age. The kingdom is here in a way that fulfills OT prophecy, yet it is not present in its consummated state. At present, Christ is ruling over the cosmos, including the whole earth, yet his rule is still contested by the powers of evil. At his return, the cosmos will be recreated and Christ will rule literally over a renewed earth and heavens. The land promise is fulfilled initially and in a real though incomplete sense as the Spirit-empowered church proclaims the kingdom throughout the earth. Its literal and complete fulfillment will occur in the recreated cosmos at Christ's return.

As believers are spiritually resurrected in this age, they begin a literal though unseen fulfillment of the resurrection prophecies of the Old Testament. In doing so, they begin to fulfil the land promises of the Old Testament in the same real, unseen, spiritual manner in which Christ presently rules the cosmos. Christians thus are identified in a real but unseen manner "with him as the new temple, new Jerusalem, new Zion, new Israel… all of which… are significant pieces of Israelite eschatological real estate" (Beale, *New Testament Biblical Theology*, p. 771). The difference between Christ and the saints is that he has been resurrected physically, and is presently reigning in heaven with a physically resurrected body, exercising his Davidic rule spiritually through his people on earth. Believers have not yet experienced this escalated fulfillment of the resurrection prophecies and along with it, possession of the land promise in a literal as well as spiritual sense. Yet they have attained possession of the land promise in a very real and present, if incomplete sense. According to the New Testament record, Christians *are now* the temple of God (1 Cor. 3:16), *are now* the inaugurated new creation (2 Cor. 5:17), *are now* the new Jerusalem, *are now* Mount Zion (Heb. 12:22) and *are now* indeed the new Israel (Gal. 6:16).

CONCLUSION

The claim of dispensationalism that a large number of highly significant Old Testament prophecies, all those pertaining to Israel and the land, are fulfilled outside of and without reference to Christ is impossible to affirm in light of the Biblical evidence. This false theological viewpoint takes the land promise to Israel out of the context in which it was given, and ruptures the seamless web of the Biblical perspective that sees the literal land promise to Israel as an important but transitory stage in the divinely-empowered progression from the first garden temple to the last. The temple of the church represents a further and far more glorious development of the land promise than that experienced by Israel, even as the covenant in Christ both fulfills and surpasses the covenant of Moses.

The need for dispensationalism to justify such a distorted view of Scripture comes from its view that God has two separate covenants, one with Jews and one with Christians, that God sent Christ to establish a Messianic kingdom in Jerusalem and that he failed in his mission, that the cross was God's Plan B, and that the church is a mere parenthesis in the bigger plan of God to fulfill his covenant with the Jews. John Nelson Darby, the originator of dispensationalism in the 1820s, had no idea how to rework Scripture in order to remove the church and return to the covenant with the Jews, until he heard of a charismatic vision given to a young lady in a prayer meeting in Scotland. The content of the vision was interpreted by Darby to represent a secret return of Christ, a concept to that point unknown in the history of the church. Darby used the vision to twist the meaning of Greek terminology in 1 Thessalonians 4 and thereby invent the idea of the rapture. Once the church was gone, God could send Christ a second time, visibly, to do what he was supposed to have done the first time, establish a literal earthly kingdom, and to restore and preside over the sacrifices in a rebuilt temple, in direct contravention to Hebrews 7-11. The thought of a Savior who died to free us from the need to perform those sacrifices now presiding over their re-institution is both ludicrous and dishonoring to his finished work.

The countless failures of dispensational interpreters to point to events in the middle east as imminent fulfillments of Biblical prophecy and signs of the rapture, along with their utter failure ever to acknowledge they were wrong, have caused the church in the North American culture and elsewhere to become a laughing stock, and have turned multitudes of younger believers away from any study of Biblical eschatology, and some away from faith itself. This is a tragedy, because our eschatology (or lack of it) affects everything we believe. And in addition, as we have tried to make clear, it both distorts and blinds us from understanding the story line of the Bible, and where we are in that story line, in the magnificent project of our God to restore all that was lost in Eden and to establish the fulfillment of the promise of a land, a land not of this earth but of eternity, not limited to a patch of middle eastern geography, but encompassing the whole of a renewed creation.

God indeed has a temple, a city and a land prepared for his people.

ABOUT THE AUTHOR

From the Toronto region. David holds three degrees in theology. He and his wife, Elaine, have planted churches in the UK and Canada. David also teaches internationally in churches, Bible colleges, leadership training centers, and the online platforms TheosUniversity and TheosSeminary. David and Elaine have eight children and nine grandchildren which, let's be honest, is an accomplishment.

NIGHT LIGHT
How to Find God in the Midst of Suffering

By David Campbell

JOY COMES IN THE MORNING. FIND HOPE IN THE NIGHT.

Why are we scared of the dark? Usually it's because we don't know what's there. Perhaps a friend? Perhaps a foe? The Bible tells us that even though we "walk through the valley of the shadow of death," God is with us. In this topical look at Christian suffering, author David Campbell reminds us that God has purpose in every season – even the painful ones. Both provocative and comprehensive, Night Light will give you a foundation of strength

OTHER TITLES BY DAVID CAMPBELL

Exodus
The Road to Freedom in a Deconstructed World

By David Campbell

No Diving
10 Ways to Avoid the Shallow End of your Faith and Go Deeper Into the Bible

By David Campbell

Landmarks
A Comprehensive Look at the Foundations of Faith

By David Campbell

Mystery Explained
A Simple Guide to Revelation

By David Campbell

*All titles available from Amazon
or from unprecedentedpress.com/shop*

www.ingramcontent.com/pod-product-compliance
Lightning Source LLC
Chambersburg PA
CBHW070431010526
44118CB00014B/1990